Look After Yourself

Your Teeth

Look After Yourself

Your Teeth

Claire Llewellyn

W

FRANKLIN WATTS
LONDON•SYDNEY

This edition 2004

Franklin Watts
96 Leonard Street
London
EC2A 4XD

Franklin Watts Australia
45-51 Huntley Street
Alexandria
NSW 2015

Copyright © Franklin Watts 2002

Series editor: Sarah Peutrill
Art director: Jonathan Hair
Design: Kirstie Billingham
Illustrations: James Evans
Photographs: Ray Moller unless
otherwise acknowledged
Picture research: Diana Morris
Series consultant: Lynn Huggins-Cooper
Dental consultant: Darren Cromey, BDS

Acknowledgments:
Paul Barton/Corbisstockmarket: 25tr.
Rick Gomez/Corbisstockmarket: 15t.
Dr. Peter Gordon/Science Photo Library: 24.
Dr. H.C. Robinson/Science Photo Library: 25b.

With thanks to our models: Aaron, Charlotte, Connor,
Jake and Nadine

A CIP record for this book is available from the British
Library.

Dewey Classification 612

ISBN: 0 7496 5649 2

Printed in Hong Kong/China

Contents

Looking at teeth

Everyone has teeth. They may be big or small, crooked or straight, close together or wide apart.

Everyone's teeth look different!

Teeth help us to eat. They chew our food into small, soft lumps that we can easily swallow.

We cannot swallow a whole banana. Our teeth break it into pieces.

Teeth also help us to talk. We use our lips and tongue around them to make many different sounds.

Everyone's teeth are a little bit different. They give us our own special smile.

You couldn't speak clearly if you didn't have teeth.

Teeth and gums

Teeth grow out of soft, pink gums. The gums support the teeth and help to hold them tightly.

Your teeth have two parts. The part you can see is called the crown. It has a strong, white coating called enamel.

Did you know that tooth enamel is the hardest thing in the body?

Tooth enamel is strong enough to crunch through apples and other hard foods.

The rest of the tooth is
hidden inside the gum.
This part is called the root.
It holds the tooth inside
the jaw.

Enamel

Crown

Gum

Root

Normally the
root of a tooth
is longer than
its crown.

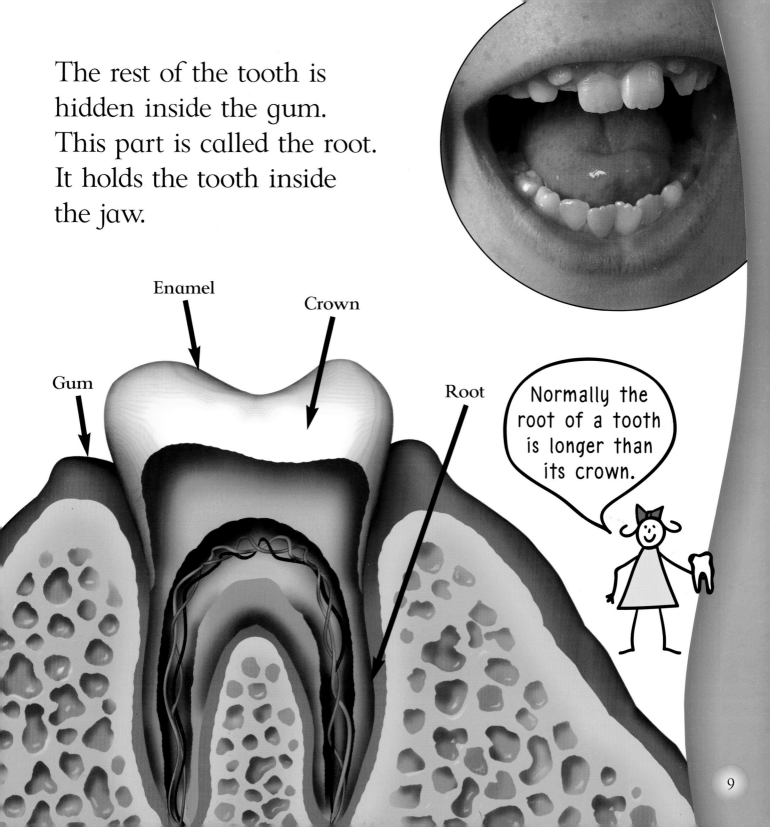

All sorts of teeth

Take a good look inside your mouth and you'll find four different kinds of teeth. Each one has its own special shape and does a different job.

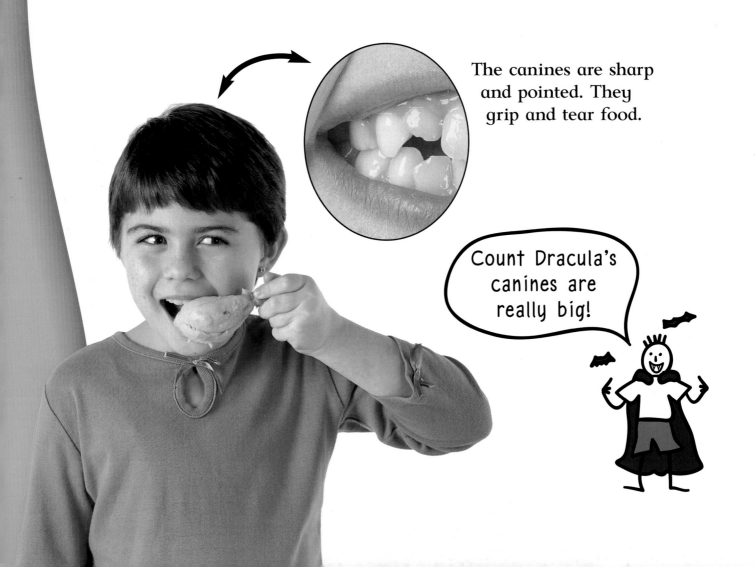

The canines are sharp and pointed. They grip and tear food.

Count Dracula's canines are really big!

Humans eat so many different foods, we need to have different kinds of teeth.

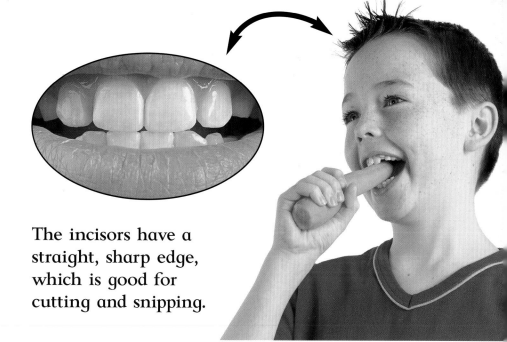

The incisors have a straight, sharp edge, which is good for cutting and snipping.

The premolars and molars are broad, flat teeth, which are good for crushing and chewing.

Meat, cereals, fruit and nuts – our teeth can deal with them all!

11

Milk teeth

When we are born we feed on milk. We do not need teeth. But teeth are hidden inside the gums and are slowly growing. They first appear when we are about six months old. They are called milk teeth.

Your milk teeth helped you to chew your first solid foods.

Between the ages of six months and two years, we grow 20 milk teeth.

As we grow bigger, our jaws grow too. We have more room for teeth. At the age of about six, new teeth grow at the back of our mouth. At the same time, the milk teeth start to drop out so that bigger ones can take their place.

How many milk teeth have you lost?

What do you do with your old milk teeth?

Adult teeth

Adult teeth are bigger than milk teeth. There are also many more of them. By the time we are about 18 years old, we have a full set of 32 teeth: 16 in the top jaw and 16 in the bottom.

How many teeth do you have? Count them and see.

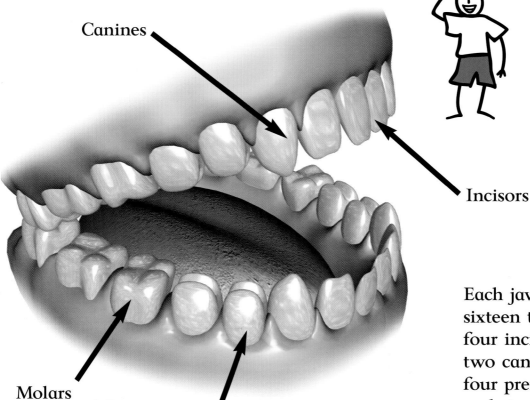

Canines

Incisors

Molars

Premolars

Each jaw contains sixteen teeth: four incisors, two canines, four premolars and six molars.

Adult teeth are big and strong, and have to last for life. It is very important to look after them.
If we lose them, they will not grow back and can never be replaced.

Adult teeth are built to last a lifetime.

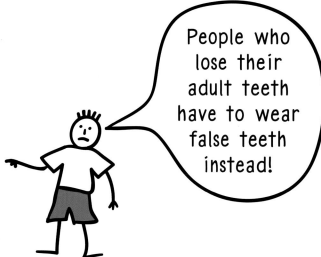

People who lose their adult teeth have to wear false teeth instead!

Food can harm teeth

Many of the foods we eat can harm our teeth. This is because some foods contain sugar or because they make sugar when they are broken down inside our mouths.

Pasta, bread and other starchy foods make sugar when they are broken down inside our mouths.

Some foods contain heaps of sugar. They are very bad for your teeth.

Some foods, such as milk and fruit, contain natural sugar.

What does the sugar do?

The sugar mixes with germs in our mouths. Germs are tiny living things that are everywhere - on our bodies, the things we touch and in the air around us. They can attack and harm us.

The mixture of sugar and germs makes an acid that rots our teeth. This causes tooth decay and leaves holes called cavities.

Tooth decay makes your teeth ache.

Brushing your teeth

You can protect your teeth from decay. Brushing twice a day helps to keep them clean. It gets rid of the germs and sugar.

Brushing makes your mouth taste good and your breath smell sweet.

Brush your teeth every morning after breakfast and before you go to bed.

1 Wet your toothbrush.

2 Put on some toothpaste (about the size of a pea).

3 Move your brush gently in circles where the teeth meet the gum. Clean every tooth on all its sides. This should take about two minutes.

How long is two minutes? Why not time yourself and see?

4 Rinse your mouth with water and spit the toothpaste out.

Cutting down on sugar

Another way of protecting your teeth is to eat less sugar. This cuts down the acid that attacks the teeth. Some foods, such as sweets and biscuits, contain more sugar than others. Why not try to choose a healthier snack?

Hard sweets like lollipops are bad for your teeth because they stay in your mouth a long time.

These foods are healthy snacks. Which ones would you like to eat?

Sweet juice or squash wash your teeth in sugar. It's better to drink water instead.

Everyone loves to eat sweet foods sometimes. Try to eat them at the end of a meal. Our mouths make a lot of saliva then, which helps to wash the sugar away.

Chewy sweets like toffee stick to the surface of your teeth. They can do a lot of harm.

Going to the dentist

The third way to protect your teeth is by going
to the dentist. Dentists examine your teeth carefully.
They check that your teeth are growing
well and that you are cleaning them properly.
They make sure there is no decay.

Visit your dentist every six months to make sure your teeth are OK!

Going to the dentist
helps to stop problems
with your teeth before
they start!

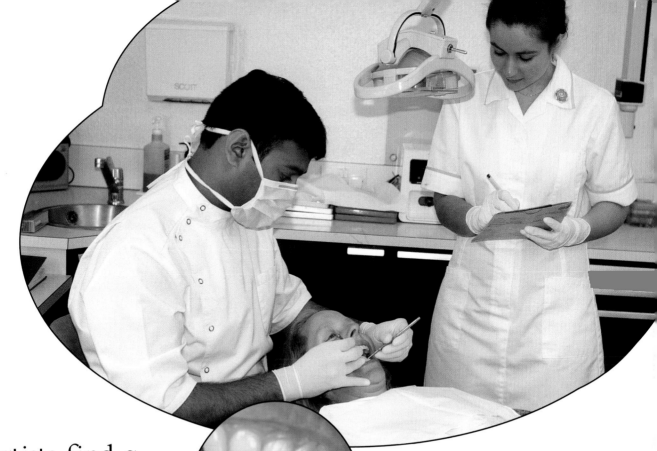

If dentists find a cavity, they fill it with metal or plastic. This stops germs getting inside the tooth and making the cavity bigger. It helps to prevent problems later on.

If it is kept clean, a filling protects your tooth and stops it decaying any more.

It's a good idea to visit the dentist. Toothache can really hurt!

A helping hand

Sometimes teeth do not grow straight.
They may grow crooked if they are very close
together. These teeth need a helping hand.

Dentists can correct crooked
teeth. They make a brace
out of thin wire and fit it
inside your mouth.

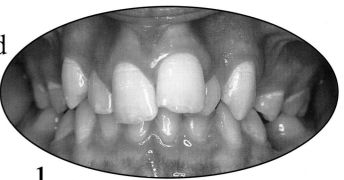

1 These teeth are crooked.

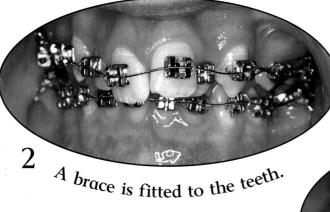

2 A brace is fitted to the teeth.

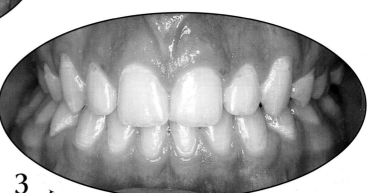

3 In time the teeth become straight.

Wearing a brace for a year or two helps to push the teeth gently into place.

Teeth can also get knocked or chipped by a fall. Dentists can repair a chipped tooth. They fit an enamel coating which looks as good as new.

Very few people have perfect teeth.

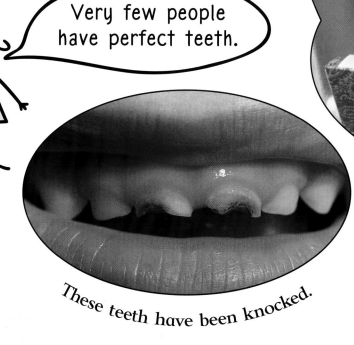

These teeth have been knocked.

Healthy teeth

Everyone wants healthy teeth. Healthy teeth look good and will last a lifetime. The food you eat helps to build your teeth. Some foods, like milk and cheese, contain calcium which helps to make teeth stronger.

Milk, cheese and other healthy foods will help to give you healthy teeth.

But foods can also damage your teeth by causing tooth decay. There are three main ways to look after your teeth:

I don't want toothache or tooth decay.

1 brush them in the morning and before you go to bed

2 cut down on sweet foods and drinks

3 visit your dentist twice a year

Your teeth are important. They belong to you. Make sure you look after them!

Glossary

acid a strong substance that attacks teeth

brace a wire frame that can be worn in the mouth to straighten teeth

calcium something found in milk and other foods which builds teeth and bones

canine the sharp, pointed tooth on each side of the incisors. We have four altogether

cavity a hole in a tooth made by tooth decay

cereals foods that are made from wheat, oats, rice and other grasses

crown the part of the tooth that is outside the gum

enamel the hard white coating on the outside of a tooth

filling the metal or plastic that is put inside a cavity to fill it and stop tooth decay

germs	tiny living things that are all around us. Some cause tooth decay
gum	the part of the mouth that holds the teeth
incisor	a tooth at the very front of the mouth that help us to cut our food. We have eight altogether
molar	a broad, flat tooth at the back of the mouth. We have 12 in all
premolar	a tooth that lies between the canines and the molars. We have eight altogether
root	the part of the tooth that grows inside the gum
saliva	the watery juice inside the mouth
surface	the top or outside of something
swallow	to move food or drink down from the mouth and into the throat
tooth decay	when teeth go bad and have holes in them

Index

About this book

Learning the principles of how to keep healthy and clean is one of life's most important skills. **Look After Yourself** is a series aimed at young children who are just beginning to develop these skills. **Your Teeth** looks at our teeth and how to care for them.

Here are a number of activities that children could try:

Pages 6-7 Use (clean!) fingers to feel their own teeth. How many do they have? What do they feel like?

Pages 8-9 Discuss how gums are just as important as the teeth themselves - the gums hold the teeth in place, and if they are not looked after properly, the teeth will fall out.

Pages 10-11 Identify each kind of tooth in their own mouths. Make a list of different foods and decide which teeth are used for eating each one (it may be more than one kind).

Pages 12-13 Do a survey of how many milk teeth each child has. Compare this with their ages.

Pages 14-15 Discuss why children have milk teeth (their jaws are too small for adult teeth).

Pages 16-17 Use disclosing tablets to find where plaque has built up.

Pages 18-19 Make teeth 'dirty' by eating some chocolate. What's the best way to clean them? Try rinsing with water, using the tongue, and brushing them.

Pages 20-21 Collect the packaging for different soft drinks. Which ones have the highest sugar content?

Pages 22-23 Make a poster to encourage children to go to the dentist.

Pages 24-25 Discuss reasons why it's usually necessary to repair broken or crooked teeth (to make it easier to eat, speak or to keep them healthy).

Pages 26-27 Think up some recipes for healthy teeth.